Real Conversations

Beginning Listening and Speaking Activities

BOOK 1

Ruth Larimer
Monterey Institute of International Studies
Monterey, California

Sherry Vaughn
Santa Rita Union School District
Salinas, California

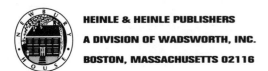

HEINLE & HEINLE PUBLISHERS
A DIVISION OF WADSWORTH, INC.
BOSTON, MASSACHUSETTS 02116

★★★

Publisher: Stanley J. Galek
Editorial Director: Christopher Foley
Project Coordinator: Talbot F. Hamlin
Assistant Editor: Erik Gundersen
Editorial Production Manager: Elizabeth Holthaus
Manufacturing Coordinator: Lisa McLaughlin
Text and Cover Design: DECODE, Inc.
Illustrations: Thomas Sperling: 1, 14, 24, 34, 50, 66;
             Precision Graphics & DECODE, Inc.: all others.

Acknowledgments

Our deep gratitude to all the people who have collected authentic conversations for us
over the last several years including:

Donna Fujimoto	Jack Holmgren	Lisa Cullen
Judy Shea	Rita Lindahl	Christie Roe
Lisa Munoz	Alice Cathcart	Tasha Doner
Janet Sharon	Cindy Casey	Pat Morales
Debbie Short	Gary Buck	Whitney Gravel

and several other doctors, dentists, employers, patients, and applicants
who have to remain nameless.

Many thanks also to those brave teachers, especially Janet Sharon and Jill DeGrange,
who tried out versions of these lessons despite partially finished pages and strange
amateur drawings. Their feedback was invaluable.

We also appreciate the anonymous reviewers who meticulously combed our pages for
activities that wouldn't work, transcripts that didn't match, and other such potential
pitfalls.

Thanks, too, to the wonderful people of Heinle and Heinle, especially Chris Foley,
Eric Gundersen, and Tab Hamlin, who worked patiently and diligently with us, always
expressing confidence and excitement about the project and most importantly, respecting
our creative control as authors.

Finally, a huge thanks for your patience during this project to:
    Jack, Rita, Alice, and Sam
who are even happier than we are to see the final version of these books.

Heinle & Heinle Publishers is a division of Wadsworth, Inc.

Manufactured in the United States of America.

ISBN 0-8384-2247-0

10 9 8 7 6 5 4 3 2 1

Contents

Introduction

Real Conversations is a two-part adult English-as-a-Second-Language (ESL) series, focusing on the development of listening and speaking skills. It is intended for adults or young adults newly arrived in the United States or those who plan to visit the United States. Book One can be used as a basic introduction to everyday conversational American English for complete beginners. Book Two includes longer, more complete conversations, often involving personal interactions such as those that take place in doctor's offices and employment interviews. All the conversations (dialogues) are completely authentic: that is, *every conversational model from the beginning of Book One is transcribed from a recording of native speakers of American English as they use the language.* The books are based on a situational syllabus, including a variety of situations for everyday conversation, as shown in the Table of Contents. Each book is accompanied by a taped reenactment of the real conversations and by a complete Instructor's Manual with detailed suggestions for use of the program.

Selection of conversation segments in *Real Conversations* is based on usefulness in the speaker's everyday life, informed by a needs assessment of 100 adult school ESL learners. Grading or ordering of conversations is based on simplicity and, in Book One, on usefulness for introducing basic vocabulary and number sets which recur in many conversations. Although the series is not structured around an item-based grammatical or functional syllabus, new and useful structures that represent the functions needed for communication in each situation are noted at the end of each unit. In Book One, many of these can be treated as idiomatic expressions to be learned as "chunks," and grammar explanation is kept to a minimum.

In *Real Conversations,* the learner is guided from listening for information in increasing stretches of discourse toward communicative activities in the classroom and community. Useful vocabulary is isolated and illustrated at the beginning of the Unit to give low-level learners a chance to get used to the sounds of the most important words used in a situation. Background for the situations is established through illustration, and the learners are led to infer meaning from context as much as possible. Activities progress from skimming and scanning for small bits of important information (such as numbers or single vocabulary items) in small stretches of conversation, to gathering information from complete brief conversations, and finally to role-playing and/or participating in information gap activities based on language used by native speakers in the models. Optional contact assignments are provided in some Units.

In Book One, the focus is on requesting various kinds of information and understanding the responses. Book One also encourages mastery of the number system, alphabet, and expressions of politeness which will recur in many survival conversations. At the beginning of several Units, there are additional "Preparation" pages for students who are completely unfamiliar with Western number or letter systems or who have extremely low listening skills. In each Unit, some functions (those to be used mainly by the native speaker and understood by the learner as consumer) are intended for comprehension while others (those to be used by the non-native speaker) are taught for production.

Using *Real Conversations*

Each Unit in *Real Conversations* is designed to lead the learner gradually towards comprehension of a conversation on a survival topic and then to performance of a simple task similar to that being performed by the native speakers. Each text is accompanied by cassette tapes which contains all the listening activities.

The cassettes include reenactments of actual conversations which were recorded by the authors in a variety of settings. These verbatim reenactments maintain the sociolinguistic elements of the original situations (age, gender, etc.) and are recorded at normal speaking rate to further bridge the gap between the classroom and the real world. Also included on the cassettes are vocabulary development and practice activities. Once the format of the lessons is familiar, the student will be able to do some of the work in a language laboratory if necessary.

Each Unit begins with a vocabulary introduction in which the student hears the new terms while looking at pictures of the items named. Students should be encouraged to "listen and look" as often as necessary before proceeding to the activities.

The activities begin with simple demonstration of vocabulary comprehension by circling pictures or matching words with pictures. Next the student identifies the vocabulary in the context of a sentence or short dialogue.

When new number sets and spelling are introduced, the "Preparation" pages referred to above precede the body of the chapter. In Book One, such preparation pages are found in Units 1, 3, 4, and 5. Students can use these pages in the laboratory, or the teacher can use them for extra practice before the numbers or letters appear in context. If students are already familiar with these items, use of the preparation pages can be omitted.

The printed word is used in *Real Conversations* mainly to familiarize students with its form and its relation to the pictures and to the spoken language they hear in the conversations. In the case of numbers, times, and money, the student responds in writing. Most activities, however, can be done without more than basic literacy.

Activities later in the Unit build familiarity with the target dialogues as students order pictures, identify a series of items, or put scrambled conversations in order. They then do simple information gap activities and perform simple speaking tasks themselves.

Directions in the student book are short, with detailed instructions in the Instructor's Manual. Teachers will want to amplify the instructions in the student books to ensure understanding. The information gap activities (in the "Partner Practice" sections), particularly require a detailed explanation and demonstration by the teacher and one student.

Step-by-step procedures and teaching suggestions for all activities are in the Instructor's Manual. The Manual should be consulted before *Real Conversations* is used.

UNIT 1

Where's the Restroom?

In Unit One, you will study:
- numbers, 1–12
- left, right, up, down, through, to;
  restroom, stairs, elevator, escalator
- "Where is …?"

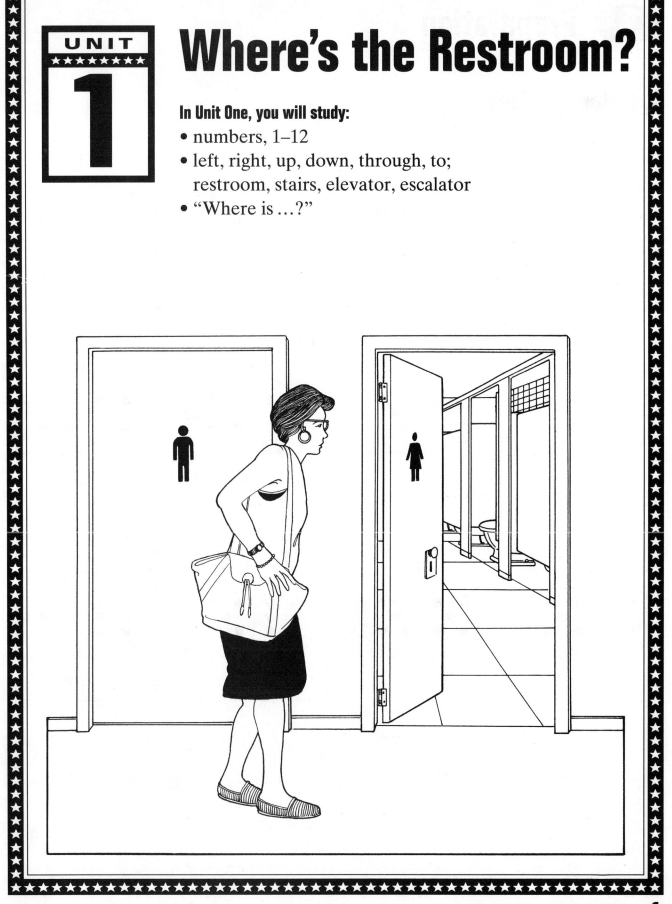

⭐1⭐ **Preparation**

A. Listen and look.

1 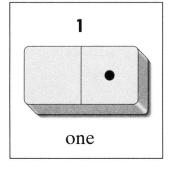 one	**2** 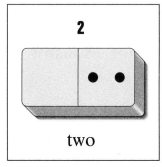 two	**3** 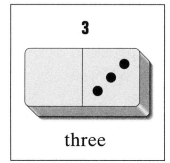 three	**4** 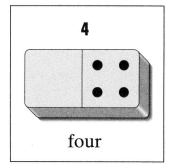 four
5 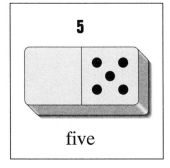 five	**6** 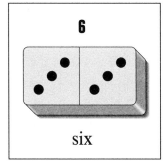 six	**7**  seven	**8** 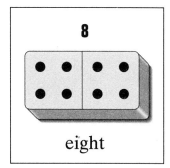 eight
9 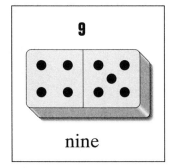 nine	**10** 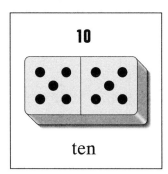 ten	**11** 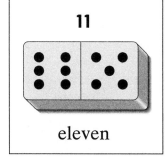 eleven	**12** 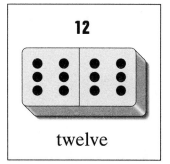 twelve

B. Practice: Listen and circle.

1.	3	(2)	1
2.	12	5	6
3.	4	10	2
4.	3	7	8
5.	8	6	11
6.	5	12	4
7.	9	7	6
8.	8	11	5
9.	7	4	10
10.	10	1	9
11.	3	2	11
12.	1	12	9

C. Practice: Listen and write.

1. _3_	**5.** _____	**9.** _____
2. _____	**6.** _____	**10.** _____
3. _____	**7.** _____	**11.** _____
4. _____	**8.** _____	**12.** _____

★2★ Vocabulary

A. Listen and look.

1. restroom

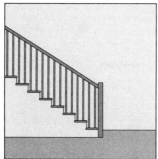

2. stairs

3. elevator

4. escalator

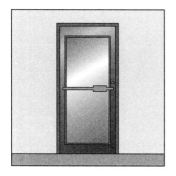

5. door

6. through the door

7. up the stairs

8. down the stairs

9. to your left

10. to your right

11. in the corner

12. in the back

B. Listen and circle.

1.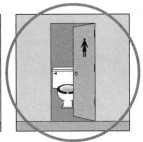

2.

3.

4.

5.

6.

7.

8.

9.

10.

11.

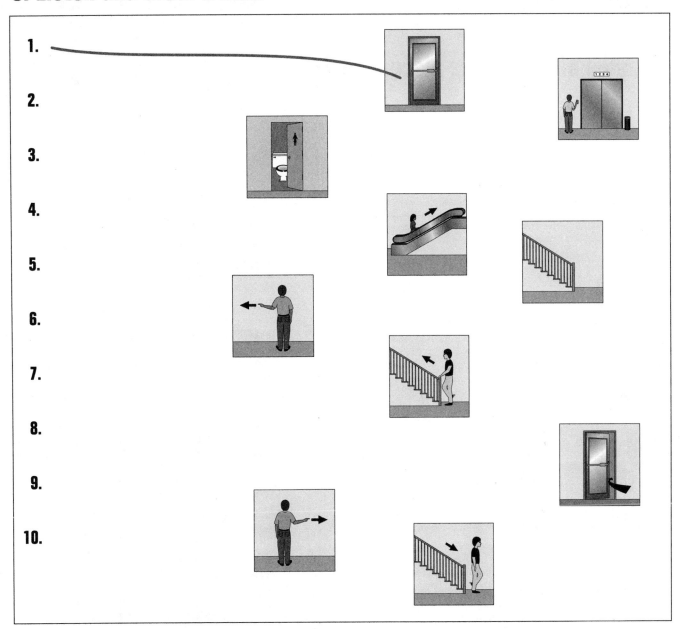

C. Listen and draw a line.

1.

2.

3.

4.

5.

6.

7.

8.

9.

10.

D. Play concentration. Use the pictures and words on Sheet A.

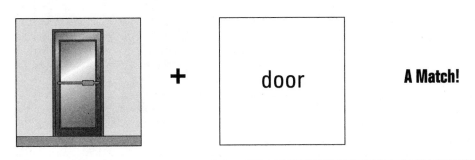

+ | door | **A Match!**

★3★ Listen to Real Conversations

A. Listen and mark the place. Use X.

1. Where's your restroom?

2. Where's your restroom?

3. Excuse me. Where's your restroom?

4. Where's the restroom?

5. Where's the nearest restroom?

6. Where's the nearest restroom?

7. Excuse me. Where's the elevator?

8. Where's the escalator?

B. Listen and practice the real conversations.

1. A: Where's your restroom?

B: *In the corner.*

2. A: Where's your restroom?

B: *It's in the back.*

3. A: Excuse me. Where's your restroom?

B: *To the left.*

4. A: Where's the restroom?

B: *Down the stairs to your left.*

5. A: Where's the nearest restroom?

B: *Up the stairs.*

6. A: Where's the nearest restroom?

B: *Through the door to your right.*

7. A: Excuse me. Where's the elevator?

B: *In the corner in the back.*

8. A: Where's the escalator?

B: *Through that door.*

Partner Practice

A. Written Conversations

Make questions. Use the words on Sheet A.

| Where | is | your | restroom | ? |

Now make answers.

| In | the | back | . |

Now put questions and answers together
to make conversations.

| Where is your restroom? |
| In the back. |

B. Talk to someone.

1. Look at the store picture.

2. Use the cut-out pictures on Sheet A.

3. Talk.

Example: A: "Excuse me. Where is the restroom?"
B: *"In the corner."*

★5★ Grammar Summary

To say:	To understand:
Where is { your restroom? the restroom? the elevator? the escalator?	*to* your left *to* your right *up* the stairs *down* the stairs *in* the corner *in* the back *through* the door
Where are the stairs?	

At the Drugstore

In Unit Two, you will study:
- numbers 1–10 in context
- drug store items (toothpaste, soap, ...)
- "is" and "are"

★★

⭐1⭐ Vocabulary

A. Listen and look.

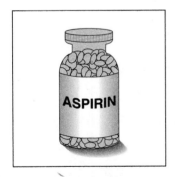

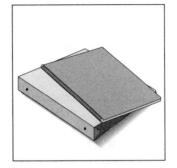

1. light bulbs

2. envelopes

3. notebooks

4. band-aids

5. shampoo

6. toothpaste

7. toilet paper

8. soap

9. aspirin

10. newspapers

11. batteries

B. Practice: Listen and circle.

1.

2.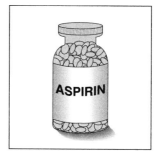

3.

4.

5.

6.

 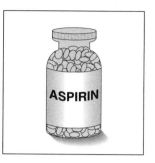 

7.

8.

9.

10.

  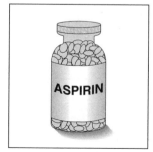

C. Listen and draw a line.

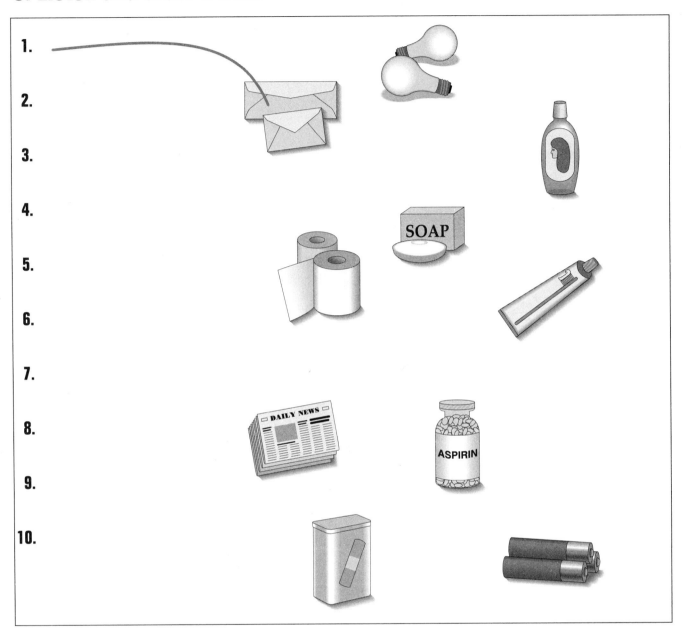

1.
2.
3.
4.
5.
6.
7.
8.
9.
10.

D. Play concentration.

+ toilet paper   **A Match!**

★2★ Listen to Real Conversations

A. Listen and write the number.

1. A: Where are the light bulbs?

B: *On aisle* ____5____ .

2. A: Where are the envelopes?

B: *In aisle* _____ .

3. A: Excuse me. Where are the newspapers?

B: *On aisle* _____ .

4. A: Excuse me. Where are the batteries?

B: *In aisle* _____ .

5. A: Pardon me. Where is the toilet paper?

B: *On aisle* _____ .

6. A: Where is the shampoo?

B: *It's on aisle* _____ .

7. A: Where is the toothpaste?

B: *It's on aisle* _____ .

B. Listen and put the pictures on the aisles.

Use Sheet B.

Example: A: "Where is the aspirin?"
B: *"On aisle 5."*

C. Listen and practice the real conversations.

1. A: Where are the light bulbs?

B: *On aisle 5.*

2. A: Where are the envelopes?

B: *In aisle 7.*

3. A: Excuse me. Where are the newspapers?

B: *On aisle 2.*

4. A: Excuse me. Where are the batteries?

B: *In aisle 9.*

5. A: Pardon me. Where is the toilet paper?

B: *On aisle 10.*

6. A: Where is the shampoo?

B: *It's on aisle 3.*

7. A: Where is the toothpaste?

B: *It's on aisle 1.*

 **Partner Practice**

A. Written conversations.

Make questions. Use the words on Sheet C.

Example: | Where | is | the | soap | ? |

Now make answers.

Example: | It's | on | aisle | 3 | . |

Now put questions and answers together to make conversations.

Example: | Where is the soap? |
| It's on aisle 3. |

B. Talk to someone.

1. Use the picture of the drugstore on page 20.

2. Use the cut-out pictures on Sheet B.

3. Talk.

   Example: A: "Excuse me. Where are the envelopes?"

   B: "On aisle 3."

★4★ Grammar Summary

To say:	To understand:
Where *is* the _____?	It *is* on aisle _____.
	It*'s* on aisle _____.
Where*'s* the { soap, toothpaste, shampoo, toilet paper, asprin	(It's *in* aisle _____.)
Where *are* the _____?	
Where*'re* the { light bulbs, envelopes, notebooks, batteries, band-aids, newspapers	They *are* on aisle _____.
	they*'re* on aisle _____.
	(They're *in* aisle _____.)

On the Street

In Unit Three, you will study:
- numbers 11–60
- excuse me, pardon me, please, thank you
- the time

⭐1⭐ **Preparation**

A. Numbers: Listen and look.

11	12	13	14
eleven	twelve	thirteen	fourteen
15	16	17	18
fifteen	sixteen	seventeen	eighteen
19	20	21	22
nineteen	twenty	twenty-one	twenty-two
23	24	25	26
twenty-three	twenty-four	twenty-five	twenty-six
27	28	29	30
twenty-seven	twenty-eight	twenty-nine	thirty
31	40	50	60
thirty-one	forty	fifty	sixty

B. Listen and circle.

1.	13	(14)	15
2.	21	31	41
3.	2	22	20
4.	16	17	26
5.	50	30	40
6.	45	55	35
7.	17	27	37
8.	13	30	40
9.	40	14	50
10.	15	50	16
11.	16	60	70
12.	13	40	30
13.	50	60	16
14.	14	50	40
15.	60	50	16
16.	50	15	40

C. Listen and write.

1. _12_

2. _____

3. _____

4. _____

5. _____

6. _____

7. _____

8. _____

9. _____

10. _____

11. _____

12. _____

13. _____

14. _____

15. _____

★★

2 **Vocabulary**

A. Listen and look.

1.

2.

3.

4.

5.

6.

7.

8.

9.

10.

11.

12.

B. Practice: Listen and circle.

1.   6:54   6:55   (6:45)   6:54

2.   10:10   12:10   2:10   12:02

3.   4:05   4:45   4:50   4:55

4.   9:33   9:23   9:44   9:53

5.   11:08   11:40   11:58   11:48

6.   10:36   1:53   1:35   1:45

7.   5:18   5:08   4:08   4:18

8.   3:52   2:52   2:42   3:42

9.   2:22   2:33   3:32   3:33

10.   7:15   7:16   6:17   6:15

★★★

C. Listen and draw a line.

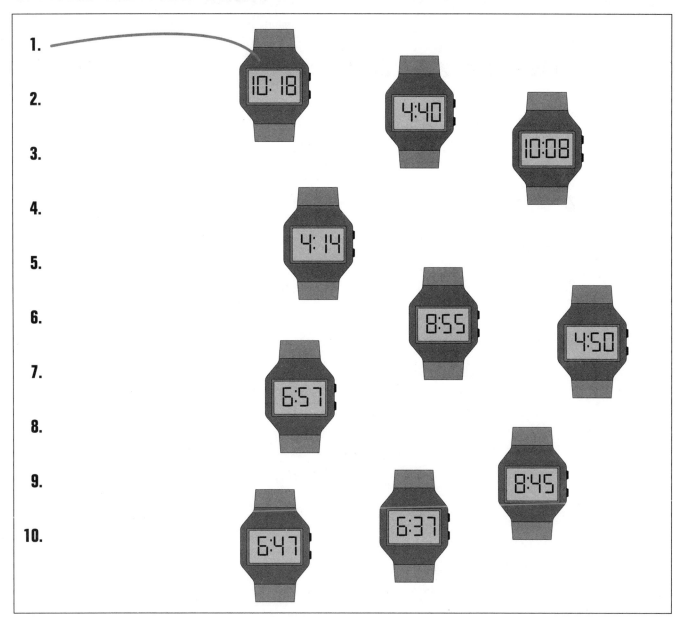

1.
2.
3.
4.
5.
6.
7.
8.
9.
10.

D. Listen and write.

1. 11:10

2. _____

3. _____

4. _____

5. _____

6. _____

7. _____

8. _____

9. _____

10. _____

★3★ Listen to Real Conversations

A. Listen and write the time.

1. A: Excuse me, do you have the time?
   B: *Yes, it's* ___11:30___ .
   A: Thanks.

2. A: What time is it, please?
   B: _____ .
   A: Thanks.

3. A: Pardon me, what time is it, please?
   B: *Um,* _____ .
   A: Okay, thanks.

4. A: Do you have the time?
   B: *Uh,* _____ *about* _____ .
   A: Thanks a lot.

5. A: Pardon me, what time is it?
   B: *It's* _____ .
   A: Thanks.

6. A: What time is it, please?
   B: *Um,* _____ .
   A: Okay, thanks.

7. A: Excuse me, do you have the time?
   B: *I have about* _____ .
   A: Thanks a lot.

8. A: Excuse me.
   B: *Uhhuh.*
   A: What time is it, please?
   B: _____ .
   A: Oh, okay, thanks

B. Listen and practice the real conversations.

1. A: Excuse me, do you have the time?
   B: *Yes, it's 12:15.*
   A: Okay, thanks.

2. A: Pardon me, do you have the time?
   B: *11:30.*
   A: Oh, okay, thanks.

3. A: What time is it, please?
   B: *8 … almost 8:40.*
   A: Thanks a lot.
   B: *Uhhuh.*

4. A: Excuse me.
   B: *Uhhuh.*
   A: What time is it, please?
   B: *Um, 5:17.*
   A: Thanks.

5. A: Excuse me, do you have the time?
   B: *No, I sure don't.*
   A: Okay, thanks.
   B: *Uhhuh.*

6. A: Do you have the time?
   B: *12:20.*
   A: Thanks.

7. A: Do you have the time?
   B: *Uh, about 12:45.*
   A: Thanks a lot.

8. A: Excuse me. Do you have the time?
   B: *I have about 10:15.*
   A: Thanks a lot.

Partner Practice

A. Written conversations.

Make conversations. Use the cut-out sentences on Sheet D.

Example: | What time is it, please? |

| Um, 5:17. |

| Oh, okay, thanks. |

B. Talk to someone.

Time
_____

1. Write a time in the box.

2. Ask 5 students the time.

3. Write their times in the chart.

Example:

A: "Pardon me, do you have the time?"

B: "Yes, it's 4:40."

A: "Thanks."

Time Chart
1. _____
2. _____
3. _____
4. _____
5. _____

⭐⭐

⭐5⭐ Try It Out

On the street.

Ask four people for the time. Write the times here.

The Time
1. _____
2. _____
3. _____
4. _____

⭐6⭐ Grammar Summary

To say:	To understand:
Excuse me, } { what time is it? Pardon me, } { do you have the time?	It's 6:25. No, I sure don't.

At the Cashier

In Unit Four, you will study:

- numbers, 60–100
- money
- "Do you have …?" and "Can I get …?"

★1★ Preparation

A. Listen and look.

60 sixty	61 sixty-one	62 sixty-two	63 sixty-three
64 sixty-four	65 sixty-five	66 sixty-six	67 sixty-seven
68 sixty-eight	69 sixty-nine	70 seventy	80 eighty
90 ninety	100 one hundred		

B. Listen and circle.

1.	77	(67)	76
2.	74	55	75
3.	68	78	58
4.	82	83	93
5.	79	99	69
6.	82	93	92
7.	66	86	96
8.	51	71	61
9.	74	73	64
10.	90	91	99
11.	76	66	56
12.	10	1	100
13.	96	69	66
14.	64	54	46
15.	70	60	50
16.	80	88	87

C. Listen and write.

1. _76_

2. _____

3. _____

4. _____

5. _____

6. _____

7. _____

8. _____

9. _____

10. _____

11. _____

12. _____

13. _____

14. _____

15. _____

D. Listen and look.

1.

    a penny
    (1 cent)

2.

    a nickel
    (5 cents)

3.

    a dime
    (10 cents)

4.

    a quarter
    (25 cents)

5.

    a dollar

6.

    five dollars

7.

    ten dollars

8.

    twenty dollars

E. Listen and circle.

1.

2.

3.

4.

5.

6.

7.

8.

★2★ Vocabulary

A. Listen and look.

1.
$4.79

2.
$11.98

3.
$23.41

4.
$15.38

5.
$ .65

6.
$ .98

7.
$9.98

8.
$6.99

9.
$12.50

10.
$10.75

11.
$3.33

12.
$2.99

13.
$6.59

14.
$13.39

15.
$1.98

B. Listen and circle.

1. $ 2.75 $ 3.25 $ 2.25 $ 3.75

2. $ 6.26 $ 8.26 $ 6.28 $ 8.66

3. $ 7.40 $ 7.00 $ 6.00 $ 7.10

4. $ 10.80 $ 8.80 $ 10.08 $ 8.08

5. $ 1.29 $ 10.29 $ 1.39 $ 10.39

6. $ 16.00 $ 60.00 $ 50.00 $ 15.00

7. $ .63 $ .68 $ .36 $ .62

8. $ .17 $ .65 $ .75 $ .74

9. $ .29 $ .39 $ .35 $ .99

10. $ .05 $ .04 $ .50 $ .15

11. $ .40 $ .50 $ .13 $ .30

12. $ 1.29 $ 1.39 $ 1.49 $ 1.13

C. Count and write.

Example:	ten	eleven	ten,	twenty,	thirty	Total

1.    **$11.30**

2.

3.

4.

5.

6.

7.

8.

9.

10.

D. Listen and draw a line.

1.

a.

2.

b.

3.

c.

4.

d.

5.

e.

6.

f.

E. Work in pairs.

1. Use the cut-out money on Sheet E.

2. Partner A is cashier. Look at Chart A and say the prices.

3. Partner B is customer. Use the cut-out money and pay.

4. Change roles. Use chart B.

Example: Partner A: "$2.42" (two forty-two)

Partner B:

Chart A	
1.	$ 2.68
2.	$ 16.57
3.	$ 11.32
4.	$ 5.45
5.	$ 22.60
6.	$ 7.28
7.	$ 18.75
8.	$ 26.20
9.	_____
10.	_____

Chart B	
1.	$ 12.30
2.	$ 3.85
3.	$ 25.46
4.	$ 13.34
5.	$ 8.28
6.	$ 28.66
7.	$ 15.83
8.	$ 9.98
9.	_____
10.	_____

★★★

⊛3⊛ Listen to Real Conversations

A. Listen and write the price or total.

1. A: Hi, _$3.75_, please.

   B: *Okay.*

2. A: _____.

   B: *Uh huh, thank you.*

3. A: _____.

   B: *Okay.*

   A: Right, thank you.

4. A: _____, please.

   B: *Okay.*

   A: Thank you.

   B: *Thank you.*

5. A: Can I have change for _____, please?

   B: *Sure.*

   A: Thank you.

6. A: Can I have change for _____, please?

   B: _____; *there you go.*

   A: Thank you.

7. A: Is that all for you?

B: *That's all, thanks.*

A: _____.

B: *Okay.*

8. A: Hi.

B: *Hi, can I get a small popcorn, please?*

A: Sure, _____.

B: *Thank you.*

9. A: Hi.

B: *Change for _____, please.*

A: There you go.

B: *Thanks.*

A: Okay.

10. A: Can I have change for _____, um, coins, four quarters?

B: *Okay, one, two, three, four, and four.*

A: Thank you.

11. A: Do you have two dimes and a nickel for _____?

B: *Sure.*

A: Thanks.

B: *Bye.*

B. Listen and look.

Is the change okay? Check "yes" or "no".

		YES	NO
1.		☐	☑
2.		☐	☐
3.		☐	☐
4.		☐	☐
5.		☐	☐
6.		☐	☐

C. Listen and practice the real conversations.

1. A: Can I have change for two dollars, please?

   B: *Two dollars, there you go.*

   A: Thank you.

2. A: Hi.

   B: *Change for a dollar, please.*

   A: There you go.

   B: *Thanks.*

   A: Okay.

3. A: Can I have change for five dollars; … coins, four quarters?

   B: *Okay, one, two, three, four, and four.*

   A: Thank you.

4. A: Do you have two dimes and a nickel for a quarter?

   B: *Sure.*

   A: Thanks.

   B: *Bye.*

5. A: Can I get change?

   B: *Sure, what do you need?*

   A: Just five ones.

★4★ Partner Practice

A. Written conversations.

Make conversations. Use the cut-out sentences on Sheet F.

Example: | Can I have change for a dollar? |

| Sure. |

| Thank you. |

B. Talk to someone.

1. Use the money pictures.

2. One partner asks for change.

3. The other partner gives the change.

Example: A: "Do you have four quarters for a dollar?"

B: "Sure." *(gives four quarters)*

★5★ Try It Out!

Go to a cashier. Ask: "Can I have change for a dollar?"
or "Can I get change, please?" What happens?

★6★ Grammar Summary

To understand:	To say:
Can I help you?	Can I have change?
	Can I get $\begin{cases} \text{change?} \\ \text{a small popcorn?} \\ \text{two nickels?} \end{cases}$

At the Reception Desk

In Unit Five, you will study:
- the alphabet
- spelling
- names, addresses and phone numbers

★1★ Preparation

A. Alphabet: Listen and look.

A a	B b	C c	D d
E e	F f	G g	H h
I i	J j	K k	L l
M m	N n	O o	P p
Q q	R r	S s	T t
U u	V v	W w	X x
	Y y	Z z	

B. Practice: Listen and circle.

1.	(A)	E	C
2.	C	Z	S
3.	E	I	A
4.	B	V	D
5.	F	S	C
6.	V	B	F
7.	G	H	J
8.	E	U	I
9.	J	H	G
10.	L	I	R
11.	I	E	M
12.	N	M	L
13.	P	B	V
14.	L	N	R
15.	N	R	M
16.	S	Z	C
17.	W	U	V
18.	Z	C	X

C. Practice: Listen and write.

1. _____ C _____

2. _____

3. _____

4. _____

5. _____

6. _____

7. _____

8. _____

9. _____

10. _____

11. _____ _____

12. _____ _____

13. _____ _____

14. _____ _____

15. _____ _____

16. _____ _____

17. _____ _____

18. _____ _____

19. _____ _____

20. _____ _____

21. _____ _____

22. _____ _____

23. _____ _____

24. _____ _____

★2★ **Vocabulary**

A. Listen and look.

1. <u>John Calvin Mack</u>
   name

2. <u>John</u>
   first name

3. <u>Calvin</u>
   middle name

4. <u>C.</u>
   middle initial

5. <u>Mack</u>
   last name

6. <u>2864 Rose Avenue, Chicago</u>
   address

7. <u>Rose Avenue</u>
   street

8. <u>Chicago</u>
   city

9. <u>60693</u>
   zip code

10. <u>(312)</u>
    area code

11. <u>446-8098</u>
    phone number

B. Listen and circle.

1.	498 Cleveland Road	624-7876	(Mary Adams)
2.	Adam Keeler	(408)	678-9012
3.	791 Arbor Street	93076	Sam Keene
4.	76 Trombone Avenue	Sandy	286-9401
5.	Kelley	R.	Jan Myers
6.	7286 Walker Street	(918)	443-7279
7.	556-4212	P.	Boston
8.	Matthew	07116	S.
9.	Samuels	363-8037	43912
10.	5891 Heath Road	Johnson	(212)

★★★

C. Practice: Listen and draw a line.

1. name ——————————— Joseph Leydon
   Joseph Laydon

2. address 785 Thomas Avenue, Gerber
   785 Thomas Avenue, Jerber

3. phone number 449-6201
   449-6021

4. name Claudia Serana
   Claudia Cerana

5. address 4811 Wheelen Road
   4811 Wheeler Road

6. last name Bomberger
   Bombarger

7. street Cowper Drive
   Cowber Drive

8. phone number (719) 682-2512
   (719) 628-2512

D. Listen and write.

1. Sa __n__ dra Down __e__ __s__

2. 478 ___ P ___ ___ er Road

3. (5 ___ 7) ___ ___ ___ - 1996

4. Lisa M ___ ___ ___ oon ___ ___

5. 592 R ___ ___ ___ ___ Avenue

6. George Ca ___ ___ ___ ___ ___ l

7. ___ 2 Gl ___ ___ ___ ___ Street, Fullbright

8. Fred ___ ___ ___ k H ___ ___ ___ land ___ ___

★★

✦3✦ Listen to Real Conversations

A. Listen and write.

1. A: And the name?
   B: Marsha _Woods_ .
   A: Okay.

2. A: And your name?
   B: _____ Morris.
   A: Do you have a middle initial?
   B: _____, Lydia.
   A: Okay

3. A: Name, please?
   B: _____ Pulido.
   A: Okay.

4. A: Okay, the address, please?
   B: ___ ___ ___ ___ Martin Drive.

5. A: Your address?
   B: ___ ___ ___ Maplewood Drive. Maplewood is one word.

6. A: May I have your phone number, please?
   B: Area code (___ ___ ___) 452-___ ___ ___ ___.
   A: Thank you.

7. A: Okay, and your address?
   B: ___ ___ ___ ___,
   A: Uhhuh.
   B: Southern Road.
   A: Okay.

8. A: Phone number.
   B: 544-___ ___ ___ ___.
   A: Okay.

B. Listen and look.

Is it right? Check "yes" or "no".

		YES	NO
1.	Tamara E. Goldstein	☑	☐
2.	Sybil Robertson	☐	☐
3.	8857 Clifton Road	☐	☐
4.	467 Hillside Drive Doylesville, 81413	☐	☐
5.	4453 Rand Street Addison, Vermont 05491	☐	☐
6.	449-7066	☐	☐
7.	(437) 698-2479	☐	☐
8.	(767) 449-6201	☐	☐

★★★

C. Listen and write the missing information.

1.

Irma   *Ryan*
FIRST   LAST

43 **74** Martin Drive
ADDRESS

544-2331
TELEPHONE

2.

Kate
FIRST   LAST

475 Bardin Road   ZIP CODE
ADDRESS

489-
PHONE NUMBER

3.

Sanchez   Michael
LAST   FIRST

2837 Grim   Avenue
ADDRESS

(712)
AREA CODE   TELEPHONE

4.

Johnson   George
LAST   FIRST   MI

    Center Street Apt.
ADDRESS

Warren   CA
CITY   STATE   ZIP

(   )   623-
AREA CODE   PHONE NUMBER

D. Listen and practice the real conversations.

1. A: Name, please.

B: *Irma I-R-M-A Ryan R-Y-A-N.*

A: Okay, the address, please.

B: *4374 Martin Drive.*

A: Phone number.

B: *544-2331.*

A: Okay.

2. A: Your name, please.

B: *Kate Brosnan B-R-O-S-N-A-N*

A: Okay, and Kate, what is your address?

B: *475 Bardin Road.*

A: Umhum, and that's 748. . .?

B: *3 2.*

A: 3 2, good, and your phone number?

B: *489-2357.*

3. A: And the name?

B: *Michael Sanchez.*

A: Address?

B: *2837 Grimsley Avenue.*

A: How do you spell your street?

B: *Grimsley, G-R-I-M-S-L-E-Y.*

A: And the phone number?

B: *Area code 712 922-5837.*

A: Okay.

4. A: I'd like to check in, and the last name is Johnson.

B: *Is that George Johnson?*

A: Yes.

B: *Do you have a middle initial?*

A: R., Ronald.

B: *Okay, and your address?*

A: 8947.

B: *8. . . ?*

A: 947 Center Street, Apartment 21, Warren, California 93097.

B: *And your phone number?*

A: (415) 623-4879.

5. A: And the name?

B: *Rathburn. R-A-T-H-B-U-R-N.*

A: O.K.

B: *O.*

A: And your address?

B: *798 Romig Road, Millbrae.*

A: OK, and the phone number?

B: *Uh, area code 312, 723-5933.*

★★

★4★ Partner Practice

A. Written conversations.

Make conversations. Use the cut-out sentences on Sheet G.

Example:

Your name, please?

John Mack, M-A-C-K.

Okay, and your address?

2864 Rose Avenue.

And the phone number?

446-8098.

B. Talk to someone.

1. Use the forms on the next page.

2. Ask three students their name, address, and phone number.

3. Write.

Example: A: "Name, please."

B: "*Myoung M-Y-O-U-N-G Kwon K-W-O-N.*"

A: "Okay, and Myoung, what
   is your address?"

B: "*609 Adams Road, Lakeview.*"

A: "And your phone number?"

B: "*Area code 507 334-5568*"

Kwon	Myoung
LAST	FIRST
609 Adams Road	
ADDRESS	
Lakeview	
CITY	
(507)	334-5568
AREA CODE	PHONE NUMBER

LAST   FIRST   MIDDLE

ADDRESS

CITY

(   )

AREA CODE   PHONE NUMBER

LAST   FIRST

ADDRESS

CITY   ZIP CODE

(   )

AREA CODE   PHONE NUMBER

LAST   FIRST   MIDDLE

ADDRESS

CITY   ZIP CODE

(   )

AREA CODE   PHONE NUMBER

★5★ Grammar Summary

To understand:

What is your $\begin{cases} \text{address?} \\ \text{middle initial?} \\ \text{zip code?} \end{cases}$

How do you spell your $\begin{cases} \text{last name?} \\ \text{street?} \end{cases}$

UNIT 6

Fast Food

In Unit Six, you will study:
- hamburger, coke, fries, …
- Can I help you?
- I'd like …, I'll have …

Hamburger 1.79
Onion Rings .65

Milk Shakes

French Fries .69 .79 .99
Soft Drinks .89 .99 1.19

★1★ Vocabulary

A. Listen and look.

1. hamburger

2. cheeseburger

3. frostie

4. milk

5. small coke

6. medium coke

7. large coke

8. small fries

9. medium fries

10. large fries

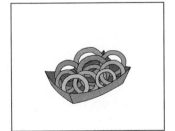

11. onion rings

12. apple pie

13. cherry pie

B. Listen and circle.

1.

2.

3.

4.

5.

6.

7.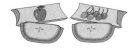

8.

9.

10.

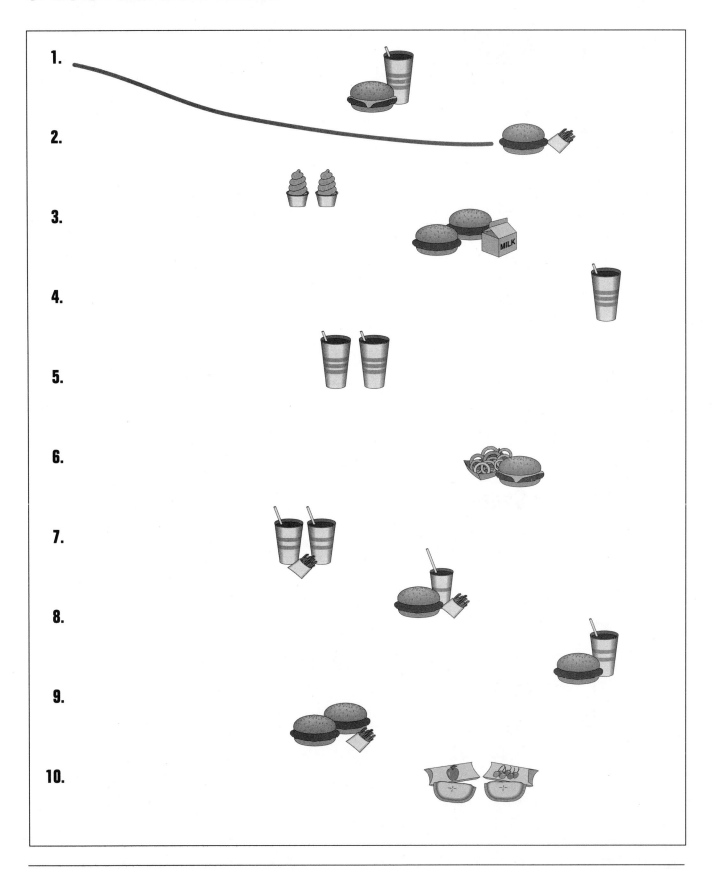

C. Listen and draw a line.

1.

2.

3.

4.

5.

6.

7.

8.

9.

10.

D. Listen and write.

1. $2.69

2. _____

3. _____

4. _____

5. _____   _____

E. Play Concentration.

Use the pictures and words on Sheets H and I.

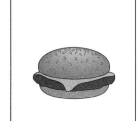 **+** | cheeseburger | **A Match!**

★★

2 Listen to Real Conversations

A. "For here or to go" Listen and circle.

	For here	To go
1.	(for here)	to go
2.	for here	to go
3.	for here	to go
4.	for here	to go
5.	for here	to go

B. Listen and write.

Price

1. _$3.75_____ , please.

2. _____ .

3. _____ .

4. _____ .

5. _____ .

Change

_$1.25_____ is your change.

_____ 's your change.

C. Listen and practice the real conversations.

1. A: Can I help you, m'am?

   B: *Okay, I'll have a hamburger and a large fries.*

   A: Okay, for here or to go?

   B: *For here.*

   A: $ 2.48, please.

   B: *Okay.*

   A: Thank you.

   B: *Thank you.*

2. A: Hi.

   B: *For here or to go?*

   A: For here. Yes. Two medium cokes.

   B: *Two medium cokes.*

   A: And one small fries.

   B: *One small fry. Will this be all?*

   A: Uh huh.

3. A: May I take your order?

   B: *Yes. Could I have a hamburger, small fries, …*

   A: hamburger, small fries …

   B: *… a medium coke, apple pie, and a cherry pie*

   A: apple pie and a cherry pie. So now you got a burger, small fries, a medium coke, apple pie, and cherry pie.

   B: *That's it.*

   A: For here or to go?

   B: *To go.*

   A: Four twenty.

   B: *Okay.*

   A: Right. Thank you.

⭐3⭐ Partner Practice

A. Written conversations.

Make conversations. Use the conversation strips on Sheet K.

Example:

| Can I help you, m'am? |

| Okay, I'll have a burger and fries. |

| Okay. For here or to go? |

| For here. |

B. Talk to someone.

1. Use the picture and money pages.
2. A has food pictures (Sheet H).
   A uses the food price chart.
3. B has money (Sheet J).
4. Talk.

Example: A: "Can I help you?"

B: "Yes, I'd like ...."

A: "For here or to go?"

B: "......."

A: "$ ...."

B: (give money)

A: "Thank you."

hamburger		$2.85
cheeseburger		$3.50
coke	small	$ .99
	medium	$1.75
	large	$2.25
fries	small	$1.25
	medium	$1.75
	large	$2.25
pies		$ .89
frosties	small	$1.15
	medium	$1.89
	large	$2.29

★★

★4★ Try it Out

Go to a fast food restaurant with a friend and order something.
Write the name of the food under #1 (or use a picture).
Write down the money you paid under #3.
Write down your change under #4.

1. Food	2. Price	3. I paid	4. My change
Example: 1.	$2.25	$3.00	$ .75
2.			

★5★ Grammar Summary

To understand:	To say:
May I help you? Can I help you? $ _____ is your change.	I'd like } I'll have } { a hamburger a cheeseburger a milk a cherry pie an apple pie a small { coke a medium { fries a large { frostie

Tapescripts

Unit 1 Tapescript

1. Preparation

Page 2. Activity A. Listen and look.

one one
two two
three three
four four
five five
six six
seven seven
eight eight
nine nine
ten ten
eleven eleven
twelve twelve

Page 3. Activity B. Listen and circle.

1. two two
2. twelve twelve
3. ten ten
4. seven seven
5. eleven eleven
6. five five
7. six six
8. eight eight
9. four four
10. nine nine
11. three three
12. one one

Page 3. Activity C. Listen and write.

1. three three
2. two two
3. six six
4. eleven eleven
5. eight eight
6. seven seven
7. four four
8. twelve twelve
9. one one
10. five five
11. nine nine
12. ten ten

2. Vocabulary

Page 4. Activity A. Listen and look.

1. restroom restroom
2. stairs stairs
3. elevator elevator
4. escalator escalator
5. door door
6. through the door through the door
7. up the stairs up the stairs
8. down the stairs down the stairs
9. to your left to your left
10. to your right to your right
11. in the corner in the corner
12. in the back in the back

Pages 5 and 6. Activity B. Listen and circle.

1. the restroom the restroom
2. the stairs the stairs
3. the escalator the escalator
4. the elevator the elevator
5. the door the door
6. up the stairs up the stairs
7. to your left to your left
8. through the door through the door
9. in the corner in the corner
10. in the back in the back
11. to your right to your right

Page 7. Activity C. Listen and draw a line.

1. Where's the door? Where's the door?
2. Where's the elevator? Where's the elevator?
3. Where's the restroom? Where's the restroom?
4. Where's the escalator? Where's the escalator?
5. Where are the stairs? Where are the stairs?
6. through the door through the door
7. to your left to your left

8. up the stairs up the stairs
9. to your right to your right
10. down the stairs down the stairs

3. Listen to Real Conversations

Pages 8 and 9. Activity A. Listen and mark the place. Use X.

1. A: Where's your restroom?
   B: *In the corner.*
2. A: Where's your restroom?
   B: *In the back.*
3. A: Excuse me. Where's your restroom?
   B: *To the left.*
4. A: Where's the restroom?
   B: *Down the stairs to your left.*
5. A: Where's the nearest restroom?
   B: *Up the stairs.*
6. A: Where's the nearest restroom?
   B: *Through the door to your right.*
7. A: Excuse me. Where's the elevator?
   B: *In the corner at the back.*
8. A: Where's the escalator?
   B: *Through that door.*

Page 10. Activity B. Listen and practice the real conversations.

Use the tapescript for Pages 8 and 9, Exercise A. Leave time to repeat after each line.

Unit 2 Tapescript

1. Vocabulary

Page 15, Activity A. Listen and look.

1. light bulbs light bulbs
2. envelopes envelopes
3. notebooks notebooks
4. band-aids band-aids
5. shampoo shampoo

6. toothpaste toothpaste
7. toilet paper toilet paper
8. soap soap
9. aspirin aspirin
10. newspapers newspapers
11. batteries batteries

Pages 16 and 17, Activity B. Listen and circle.

1. envelopes envelopes
2. shampoo shampoo
3. aspirin aspirin
4. toilet paper toilet paper
5. batteries batteries
6. band-aids band-aids
7. light bulbs light bulbs
8. notebooks notebooks
9. toothpaste toothpaste
10. newspapers newspapers

Page 18, Activity C. Listen and draw a line.

1. Where are the envelopes?
   Where are the envelopes?
2. Where are the light bulbs?
   Where are the light bulbs?
3. Where is the toilet paper?
   Where is the toilet paper?
4. Where is the shampoo?
   Where is the shampoo?
5. Where is the soap? Where is the soap?
6. Where is the aspirin? Where is the aspirin?
7. Where are the newspapers?
   Where are the newspapers?
8. Where is the toothpaste?
   Where is the toothpaste?
9. Where are the batteries?
   Where are the batteries?
10. Where are the band-aids?
    Where are the band-aids?

2. Listen to Real Conversations

Page 19, Activity A. Listen and write the number.

1. A: Where are the light bulbs?
   B: *On aisle 5.*
2. A: Where are the envelopes?
   B: *In aisle 7.*

3. A: Excuse me. Where are the newspapers?
   B: *On aisle 2.*
4. A: Excuse me. Where are the batteries?
   B: *In aisle 9.*
5. A: Pardon me. Where is the toilet paper?
   B: *On aisle 10.*
6. A: Where is the shampoo?
   B: *It's on aisle 3.*
7. A: Where is the toothpaste?
   B: *It's on aisle 1.*

Page 20, Activity B. Listen and put pictures on the aisles.

Use the same script as in exercise A, above.

Page 21, Activity C. Listen and practice the real conversations.

Use the same script as in exercises A and B.

Unit 3 Tapescript

1. Preparation

Page 25, Activity A, Numbers. Listen and look.

11, 11	19, 19	27, 27
12, 12	20, 20	28, 28
13, 13	21, 21	29, 29
14, 14	22, 22	30, 30
15, 15	23, 23	31, 31
16, 16	24, 24	40, 40
17, 17	25, 25	50, 50
18, 18	26, 26	60, 60

Page 26, Activity B. Listen and circle.

1. 14, 14	9. 40, 40
2. 41, 41	10. 50, 50
3. 22, 22	11. 16, 16
4. 17, 17	12. 13, 13
5. 50, 50	13. 60, 60
6. 45, 45	14. 14, 14
7. 37, 37	15. 50, 50
8. 13, 13	16. 15, 15

Page 26, Activity C. Listen and write.

1. 12, 12	9. 19, 19
2. 31, 31	10. 36, 36
3. 20, 20	11. 45, 45
4. 48, 48	12. 30, 30
5. 17, 17	13. 39, 39
6. 27, 27	14. 18, 18
7. 16, 16	15. 32, 32
8. 43, 43	

2. Vocabulary

Page 27, Activity A. Listen and look.

1. one o'clock, one o'clock
2. five o'clock, five o'clock
3. eight o'clock, eight o'clock
4. eleven o'clock, eleven o'clock
5. three thirty, three thirty
6. two thirty, two thirty
7. six fifteen, six fifteen
8. four forty-five, four forty-five
9. nine o seven, nine o seven
10. ten twenty-eight, ten twenty-eight
11. seven fifty-five, seven fifty-five
12. twelve thirty-eight, twelve thirty-eight

Page 28, Activity B. Listen and circle.

1. six forty-five, six forty-five
2. twelve ten, twelve ten
3. four o five, four o five
4. nine twenty-three, nine twenty-three
5. eleven forty-eight, eleven forty-eight
6. one thirty-five, one thirty-five
7. five eighteen, five eighteen
8. two fifty-two, two fifty-two
9. three thirty-three, three thirty-three
10. seven fifteen, seven fifteen

Page 29, Activity C. Listen and draw a line.

1. ten eighteen, ten eighteen
2. four forty, four forty
3. four fourteen, four fourteen
4. ten o eight, ten o eight
5. four fifty, four fifty
6. six fifty-seven, six fifty-seven
7. eight fifty-five, eight fifty-five

8. six thirty-seven, six thirty-seven
9. eight forty-five, eight forty-five
10. six forty-seven, six forty-seven

Page 29, Activity D. Listen and write.

1. eleven ten, eleven ten
2. nine thirteen, nine thirteen
3. two fifty-four, two fifty-four
4. eight o five, eight o five
5. twelve fifteen, twelve fifteen
6. three thirty, three thirty
7. six twenty, six twenty
8. one forty-one, one forty-one
9. five twenty, five twenty
10. ten ten, ten ten

3. Listen to Real Conversations

Page 30, Activity A. Listen and write the time.

1. A: Excuse me, do you have the time?
   B: *Yes, it's eleven thirty.*
   A: Thanks.
2. A: What time is it, please?
   B: *Seven thirty-nine.*
   A: Thanks.
3. A: Pardon me, what time is it, please?
   B: *Um, three forty.*
   A: Okay, thanks.
4. A: Do you have the time?
   B: *Uh, twelve......about twelve twenty-five.*
   A: Thanks a lot.
5. A: Pardon me, what time is it?
   B: *It's four thirty.*
   A: Thanks.
6. A: What time is it, please?
   B: *Um, seven forty-eight.*
   A: Okay, thanks.
7. A: Excuse me, do you have the time?
   B: *I have about ten fifteen.*
   A: Thanks a lot.
8. A: Excuse me.
   B: *Uhhuh.*
   A: What time is it, please?
   B: *Five o'clock.*
   A: Oh, okay, thanks.

Page 31, Activity B. Listen and practice the real conversations.

1. A: Excuse me, do you have the time?
   B: *Yes, it's twelve fifteen.*
   A: Okay, thanks.
2. A: Pardon me, do you have the time?
   B: *Eleven thirty.*
   A: Oh, okay, thanks.
3. A: What time is it, please?
   B: *Eight.....almost eight forty.*
   A: Thanks a lot.
   B: *Uhhuh.*
4. A: Excuse me.
   B: *Uhhuh.*
   A: What time is it, please?
   B: *Um, five seventeen.*
   A: Thanks.
5. A: Excuse me, do you have the time?
   B: *No, I sure don't.*
   A: Okay, thanks.
   B: *Uhhuh.*
6. A: Do you have the time?
   B: *Twelve twenty.*
   A: Thanks.
7. A: Do you have the time?
   B: *Uh, about twelve forty-five.*
   A: Thanks a lot.
8. A: Excuse me. Do you have the time?
   B: *I have about ten fifteen.*
   A: Thanks a lot.

Unit 4 Tapescript

1. Preparation

Page 35, Activity A. Listen and look.

sixty, sixty
sixty-one, sixty-one
sixty-two, sixty-two
sixty-three, sixty-three
sixty-four, sixty-four
sixty-five, sixty-five
sixty-six, sixty-six
sixty-seven, sixty-seven
sixty-eight, sixty-eight
sixty-nine, sixty-nine
seventy, seventy
eighty, eighty
ninety, ninety
one hundred, one hundred

Page 36, Activity B. Listen and circle.

1. sixty-seven, sixty-seven
2. seventy-five, seventy-five
3. sixty-eight, sixty-eight
4. eighty-three, eighty-three
5. seventy-nine seventy-nine
6. ninety-two, ninety-two
7. eighty-six eighty-six
8. sixty-one, sixty-one
9. seventy-four, seventy-four
10. ninety, ninety
11. fifty-six, fifty-six
12. one hundred, one hundred
13. ninety-six, ninety-six
14. fifty-four, fifty-four
15. sixty, sixty
16. eighty-eight, eighty-eight

Page 36, Activity C. Listen and write.

1. seventy-six, seventy-six
2. ninety-three, ninety-three
3. one hundred, one hundred
4. eighty-five, eighty-five
5. sixty-seven, sixty-seven
6. ninety-one, ninety-one
7. eighty-nine, eighty-nine
8. sixty-two, sixty-two
9. seventy-eight, seventy-eight
10. ninety-four, ninety-four
11. seventy-one, seventy-one
12. eighty-six, eighty-six
13. sixty-five, sixty-five
14. fifty-three, fifty-three
15. sixty-seven, sixty-seven

Page 37, Activity D. Listen and look.

1. a penny, a penny (pause) or one cent, one cent
2. a nickel, a nickel (pause) or five cents, five cents
3. a dime, a dime (pause) or ten cents, ten cents
4. a quarter, a quarter (pause) or twenty-five cents, twenty-five cents
5. a dollar, a dollar
6. five dollars, five dollars
7. ten dollars, ten dollars
8. twenty dollars, twenty dollars

Page 38, Activity E. Listen and circle.

1. a nickel, a nickel
2. a quarter, a quarter
3. ten cents, ten cents
4. a penny, a penny
5. five cents, five cents
6. ten dollars, ten dollars
7. one cent, one cent
8. twenty dollars, twenty dollars

2. Vocabulary

Page 39, Activity A. Listen and look.

1. four seventy-nine, four seventy-nine
2. eleven ninety-eight, eleven ninety-eight
3. twenty-three forty-one, twenty-three forty-one
4. fifteen thirty-eight, fifteen thirty-eight
5. sixty-five cents, sixty-five cents,
6. ninety-eight cents, ninety-eight cents
7. nine ninety-eight, nine ninety-eight
8. six ninety-nine, six ninety-nine
9. twelve fifty, twelve fifty
10. ten seventy-five, ten seventy-five
11. three thirty-three, three thirty-three
12. two ninety-nine, two ninety-nine
13. six fifty-nine, six fifty-nine
14. thirteen thirty-nine, thirteen thirty-nine
15. one ninety-eight one ninety-eight

Page 40, Activity B. Listen and circle.

1. three seventy-five, three seventy-five
2. eight twenty-six, eight twenty-six
3. seven dollars, seven dollars
4. ten o eight, ten o eight
5. one twenty-nine one twenty-nine
6. fifty dollars, fifty dollars
7. sixty-three cents, sixty-three cents
8. seventy-five cents, seventy-five cents
9. twenty-nine cents, twenty-nine cents
10. five cents, five cents
11. thirty cents, thirty cents
12. one dollar and thirty-nine cents, one dollar and thirty-nine cents

Page 42, Activity D. Listen and draw a line.

1. two sixty-nine, two sixty-nine
2. four forty-two, four forty-two
3. three seventy-six, three seventy-six
4. eight fifty-three, eight fifty-three
5. seven forty-five, seven forty-five
6. four sixty-six, four sixty-six

3. Listen to Real Conversations

Pages 44 and 45, Activity A. Listen and write the price or total.

1. A: Hi, three seventy-five, please.
   B: *Okay.*
2. A: Forty-seven cents.
   B: *Uh huh, thank you.*
3. A: Four twenty.
   B: *Okay.*
   A: Right, thank you.
4. A: Two forty-eight, please.
   B: *Okay.*
   A: Thank you.
   B: *Thank you.*
5. A: Can I have change for ten dollars, please?
   B: *Sure.*
   A: Thank you.
6. A: Can I have change for two dollars, please?
   B: *Two dollars, there you go.*
   A: Thank you.
7. A: Is that all for you?
   B: *That's all, thanks.*
   A: Twenty-four fifty.
   B: *Okay.*
8. A: Hi.
   B: *Hi, can I get a small popcorn, please.*
   A: Sure, fifty cents.
   B: *Thank you.*
9. A: Hi.
   B: *Change for a dollar, please.*
   A: There you go.
   B: *Thanks.*
   A: Okay.
10. A: Can I have change for five dollars, um, coins, four quarters?
    B: *Okay, one, two, three, four, and four.*
    A: Thank you.
11. A: Do you have two dimes and a nickel for a quarter?
    B: *Sure.*
    A: Thanks.
    B: *Bye.*

Page 46, Activity B. Listen and look. Is the change okay?

1. A: Can I have change for two dollars, please?
   B: *Two dollars, there you go.*
   A: Thank you.
2. A: Hi.
   B: *Change for a dollar, please.*
   A: There you go.
   B: *Thanks.*
   A: Okay.
3. A: Can I have change for five dollars, um, coins, four quarters?

B: *Okay, one, two three, four, and four.*
A: Thank you.
4. A: Do you have two dimes and a nickel for a quarter?
    B: *Sure.*
    A: Thanks.
    B: *Bye.*
5. A: Can I get change?
    B: *Sure, what do you need?*
    A: Just, uh, five ones.
6. A: Can I help you?
    B: *Yep, I'm gonna need change, All I have is a five dollar bill.*
    A: Okay.
    B: *Thank you very much.*

Page 47, Activity C. Listen and practice the real conversations.

1. A: Can I have change for two dollars, please?
    B: *Two dollars, there you go.*
    A: Thank you.
2. A: Hi.
    B: *Change for a dollar, please.*
    A: There you go.
    B: *Thanks.*
    A: Okay.
3. A: Can I have change for five dollars, um, coins, four quarters?
    B: *Okay, one, two, three, four, and four.*
    A: Thank you.
4. A: Do you have two dimes and a nickel for a quarter?
    B: *Sure.*
    A: Thanks.
    B: *Bye.*
5. A: Can I get change?
    B: *Sure, what do you need?*
    A: Just, uh, five ones.

Unit 5 Tapescript

1. Preparation

Page 51, Activity A, Alphabet. Listen and look.

1. A, A	14. N, N
2. B, B	15. O, O
3. C, C	16. P, P
4. D, D	17. Q, Q
5. E, E	18. R, R
6. F, F	19. S, S
7. G, G	20. T, T
8. H, H	21. U, U
9. I, I	22. V, V
10. J, J	23. W. W
11. K, K	24. X, X
12. L, L	25. Y, Y
13. M, M	26. Z, Z

Page 52, Activity B. Listen and circle.

1. A, A	10. R, R
2. Z, Z	11. E, E
3. E, E	12. N, N
4. V, V	13 B, B
5. S, S	14. L, L
6. F, F	15. N, N
7. G, G	16. C, C
8. I, I	17. V, V
9. J, J	18. X, X

Page 53, Activity C, Listen and write.

1. C, C	13. T.O, T.O
2. B, B	14. I.R, I.R
3. F, F	15. D.L, D.L
4. G, G	16. E.C, E.C
5. M, M	17. F.G, F.G
6. L, L	18. M.A, M.A
7. E, E	19. K.H, K.H
8. N, N	20. U.I, U.I
9. P, P	21. J.P, J.P
10. R, R	22. N.O, N.O
11. M.E, M.E	23. T.N, T.N
12. S.A, S.A	24 O.W, O.W

2. Vocabulary

Page 54, Activity A. Listen and look.

1. –Name
    –John Calvin Mack
2. –First name
    –John

3. –Middle name
    –Calvin
4. –Middle initial
    –C.
5. –Last name
    –Mack
6. –Address
    –2864 Rose Avenue, Chicago
7. –Street
    –Rose Avenue
8. –City
    –Chicago
9. –Zip code
    –60693
10. –Area code
    –312
11. –Phone number
    –446-8098

Page 55, Activity B. Listen and circle.

1. Name:
    498 Cleveland Road,
    624-7876,
    Mary Adams.
2. Phone number:
    Adam Keeler,
    (408),
    678-9012.
3. Address:
    791 Arbor Street,
    93076,
    Sam Keene.
4. First name:
    76 Trombone Avenue,
    Sandy, 286-9401.
5. Middle Initial:
    Kelley,
    R.,
    Jan Myers.
6. Area code:
    7286 Walker Street,
    (918),
    443-7279.
7. City:
    556-4212,
    P.,
    Boston.
8. Middle name:
    Matthew,
    07116,
    S.

9. Zip code:
   Samuels,
   363-8037,
   43912.
10. Last name:
    5891 Heath Road,
    Johnson,
    (212).

Page 56, Activity C. Listen and draw a line.

1. A: Name?
   B: *Joseph Leydon, L-e-y-d-o-n.*
2. A: Address?
   B: *785 Thomas Avenue, Gerber, G-e-r-b-e-r.*
3. A: Phone number?
   B: *449-6201.*
4. A: Name?
   B: *Claudia Serana, S-e-r-a-n-a.*
5. A: Address?
   B: *4811 Wheeler, W-h-e-e-l-e-r Road.*
6. A: Last name?
   B: *Bomberger, B-o-m-b-e-r-g-e-r.*
7. A: Street?
   B: *Cowper Drive C-o-w-p-e-r.*
8. A: Phone number?
   B: *(719) 628-2512.*

Page 57. Activity D, Listen and write.

1. A: Name?
   B: *Sandra, S-a-n-d-r-a Downes, D-o-w-n-e-s.*
2. A: Address?
   B: *4782 Piper, P-i-p-e-r Road.*
3. A: Phone number?
   B: *(537) 984-1996.*
4. A: Name?
   B: *Lisa Mulrooney, M-u-l-r-o-o-n-e-y.*
5. A: Address?
   B: *592 Reese, R-e-e-s-e Avenue.*
6. A: Name?
   B: *George Campbell, C-a-m-p-b-e-l-l.*
7. A: Address?
   B: *42 Gleeson, G-l-e-e-s-o-n Street, Fullbright.*
8. A: Name?
   B: *Frederick, F-r-e-d-e-r-i-c-k Highlander, H-i-g-h-l-a-n-d-e-r.*

3. Listen to Real Conversations

Page 58, Activity A. Listen and write.

1. A: And the name?
   B: *Marsha, M-a-r-s-h-a Woods W-o-o-d-s.*
   A: Okay.
2. A: And your name?
   B: *Teresa T-e-r-e-s-a Morris.*
   A: Uhm, do you have a middle initial?
   B: *L, Lydia.*
   A: Okay.
3. A: Name, please?
   B: *Jamie J-a-m-i-e Pulido, P-u-l-i-d-o.*
   A: Okay.
4. A: Okay, the address, please?
   B: *Four-three-seven-three Martin Drive.*
5. A: Your address?
   B: *Nine zero seven Maplewood Drive. Maplewood is one word.*
6. A: May I have your phone number please?
   B: *Area code 618, 452-7968.*
7. A: Okay, and your address?
   B: *One four nine five,*
   A: uhhuh,
   B: *Southern Road.*
   A: Okay.
8. A: Phone number?
   B: *544-2331.*
   A: Okay.

Page 59, Activity B. Listen and look. Is it right?

1. A: Your name, please?
   B: *Tamara, T-a-m-a-r-a Goldstein G-o-l-d-s-t-e-i-n.*
   A: And Tamara, do you have a middle initial?
   B: *E, Elizabeth.*
   A: Okay.
2. A: And your name?
   B: *Sybil, S-y-b-i-l Roberson.*
   A: R-o-b?
   B: *e-r-s-o-n.*
   A: Roberson, okay.
3. A: The address?
   B: *eighty-eight fifty-four Clifden, C-l-i-f-d-e-n Road.*
   A: Okay.

4. A: Okay, the address please?
   B: *Four sixty seven,*
   A: Uhhuh,
   B: *Hillside Drive, in Doylesville.*
   A: And what's your zip out there.
   B: *81143.*
5. A: And what's your address?
   B: *4553 Rand Street,*
   A: Uhhuh,
   B: *Addison, Vermont,*
   A: Uhhuh,
   B: *05491.*
   A: Okay.
6. A: Phone number?
   B: *449-7-zero-zero 6.*
   A: 449-7-zero-zero 6.
7. A: Your phone number?
   B: *(437) 698-2479.*
8. A: The phone number?
   B: *Area code 767, 449-6 oh 21. Let me just look it up to make sure. . . umhum.*

Page 60, Activity C. Listen and write the missing information.

1. A: Name, please?
   B: *Irma I-R-M-A Ryan R-Y-A-N.*
   A: Okay, the address, please?
   B: *4374 Martin Drive.*
   A: Phone number?
   B: *544-2331.*
   A: Okay.
2. A: Your name, please?
   B: *Kate Brosnan B-R-O-S-N-A-N.*
   A: Okay, and Kate, what is your address?
   B: *475 Bardin Road.*
   A: Umhum, and that's 748. . . .?
   B: *3 2.*
   A: 32, good, and your phone number?
   B: *489-2357.*
3. A: And the name?
   B: *Michael Sanchez.*
   A: Address?
   B: *2837 Grimsley Avenue.*
   A: How do you spell your street?
   B: *Grimsley, G-R-I-M-S-L-E-Y.*

A: And the phone number?
B: *Area code 712 922-5837.*
A: Okay.
4. A: I'd like to check in, and the last name is Johnson.
  B: *Is that George Johnson?*
  A: Yes.
  B: *Do you have a middle initial?*
  A: R., Ronald.
  B: *Okay, and your address?*
  A: 8947,
  B: *8. . . ?*
  A: 947 Center Street, Apartment 21, Warren, California 9-3-zero-9-7.
  B: *And your phone number?*
  A: 415 623-4879.

Pages 61 and 62, Activity D. Listen and practice the real conversations.

1. A: Name, please?
  B: *Irma I-R-M-A Ryan R-Y-A-N.*
  A: Okay, the address, please.
  B: *4374 Martin Drive.*
  A: Phone number?
  B: *544-2331.*
  A: Okay.
2. A: Your name, please?
  B: *Kate Brosnan B-R-O-S-N-A-N.*
  A: Okay, and Kate, what is your address?
  B: *475 Bardin Road.*
  A: Umhum, and that's 748. . .?
  B: *3 2.*
  A: 32, good, and your phone number?
  B: *489-2357.*
3. A: And the name?
  B: *Michael Sanchez.*
  A: Address?
  B: *2837 Grimsley Avenue.*
  A: How do you spell your street?
  B: *Grimsley, G-R-I-M-S-L-E-Y.*
  A: And the phone number?
  B: *Area code 712 922-5837.*
  A: Okay.

4. A: I'd like to check in, and the last name is Johnson.
  B: *Is that George Johnson?*
  A: Yes.
  B: *Do you have a middle initial?*
  A: R., Ronald.
  B: *Okay, and your address?*
  A: 8947,
  B: *8. . . ?*
  A: 947 Center Street, Apartment 21, Warren, California 9-3-zero-9-7.
  B: *And your phone number?*
  A: 415 623-4879.
5. A: And the name?
  B: *Rathburn. R-A-T-H-B-U-R-N.*
  A: Okay.
  B: *O.*
  A: And your address?
  B: *798 Romig Road, Millbrae.*
  A: Okay, and the phone number?
  B: *Uh, area code 312, 723-5933.*

Unit 6 Tapescript

1. Vocabulary

Page 67, Activity A. Listen and look.

1. hamburger (pause) or burger, hamburger (pause) or burger
2. cheeseburger, cheeseburger
3. frostie, frostie
4. milk, milk
5. small coke, small coke
6. medium coke, medium coke
7. large coke, large coke
8. small fries, small fries
9. medium fries, medium fries
10. large fries, large fries
11. onion rings, onion rings
12. apple pie, apple pie
13. cherry pie, cherry pie

Page 68, Activity B. Listen and circle.

1. a small fries, a small fries
2. a medium coke, a medium coke
3. two small frosties, two small frosties
4. a cheeseburger, a cheeseburger
5. a large fries, a large fries
6. two medium cokes, two medium cokes
7. a cherry pie, a cherry pie
8. a cheeseburger and a coke, a cheeseburger and a coke
9. a small fries and a frostie, a small fries and a frostie
10. onion rings and a coke, onion rings and a coke

Page 69, Activity C. Listen and draw a line.

1. a hamburger and small fries, a hamburger and small fries
2. a cheeseburger and a large coke, a cheeseburger and a large coke
3. two small frosties, two small frosties
4. two hamburgers and one milk, two hamburgers and one milk
5. two large cokes, two large cokes
6. a cheeseburger and onion rings, a cheeseburger and onion rings
7. two medium cokes and one small fries, two medium cokes and one small fries
8. a burger, a small fries and a coke; a burger, a small fries and a coke
9. apple pie and a cherry pie, apple pie and a cherry pie
10. two burgers and a small fries, two burgers and a small fries

Page 70, Activity D. Listen and write.

1. Two sixty-nine, please.
2. Four twenty.
3. That comes to three seventy five.
4. One twenty-five is your change.
5. A: Two fifty-nine.
  B: *Okay.*
  A: One cent's your change.

2. Listen to Real Conversations

Page 71, Activity A, "For here or to go." Listen and circle.

1. A: Hi.
   B: For here or to go?
   A: For here, yeh, two small frosties.
2. A: So you got a burger, small fries and a medium coke.
   B: That's right.
   A: For here or to go?
   B: To go.
3. A: That's it?
   B: Yeh.
   A: Okay, all of them to go?
   B: Yeh, all to go.
4. A: A hamburger and a large fries.
   B: Okay, for here or to go?
   A: For here.
5. A: Okay, that's it.
   B: For here or to go?
   A: To go.

Page 71, Activity B. Listen and write.

1. A: Three seventy-five, please.
   B: Okay.
   A: One twenty-five is your change.
   B: Thank you.
2. A: Three twenty-nine.
   B: Okay.
   A: One cent's your change.
   B: Okay, thank you.
3. A: Two twenty-five.
   B: Okay.
   A: Right. Thank you.
4. A: For here or to go?
   B: For here.
   A: Two forty-eight, please.
   B: Okay.
   A: Thank you.
5. A: That's it.
   B: Okay. That's four twenty.
   A: Okay.
   B: Right

Page 72. Activity C. Listen and practice the real conversations.

1. A: Can I help you, m'am?
   B: Okay, I'll have a hamburger and a large fries.

A: Okay, for here or to go?
B: For here.
A: Two forty-eight, please.
B: Okay.
A: Thank you.
B: Thank you.
2. A: Hi.
   B: For here or to go?
   A: For here.
   Yes. Two medium cokes.
   B: Two medium cokes.
   A: And one small fries.
   B: One small fry.
   Will this be all?
   A: Uh huh.
3 A: May I take your order?
   B: Yes. Could I have a hamburger, small fries,
   A: hamburger, small fries,
   B: . . . a medium coke, apple pie, and a cherry pie.
   A: apple pie and a cherry pie. So now you got a burger, small fries, a medium coke, apple pie, and cherry pie.
   B: That's it.
   A: For here or to go?
   B: To go.
   A: Four twenty.
   B: Okay.
   A: Right. Thank you.

Unit 1: Sheet A

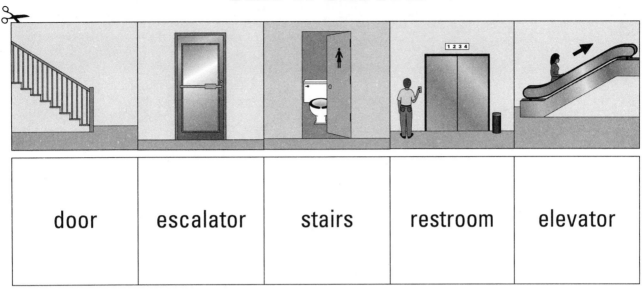

door	escalator	stairs	restroom	elevator

1

restroom	your	Where's	?	?	?	elevator

Where	's	escalator	the	Where	the	is

the	is	Where

2

the	the	the	in	In	back	corner	to

to	left	right	the	me	the	.	Excuse

through	door	down	up	your	stairs	stairs

the	to	left	.

Unit 2: Sheet B

	envelopes	toothpaste	aspirin	notebooks
shampoo	newspapers	toilet paper	batteries	light bulbs
band-aids	soap			

Unit 2: Sheet C

1

the	Where	band-aids	are	?	is	soap

the	Where	?	?	toothpaste	is	Where

the	the	Where's	shampoo	?

2

on	It's	aisle	3	2	5	aisle	on	It's

aisle	on	in	7	aisle	They're	.	.	.

in	10	aisle

Sample

Um, about 3:15.

What time is it, please? | Oh, okay, thanks.

1

Yes, it's 12:15. | Okay, thanks.

Excuse me, do you have the time?

2

Oh, okay, thanks. | 11:30.

Pardon me, do you have the time?

3

Uh huh. | 8 … almost 8:40.

What time is it, please? | Thanks a lot.

4

Um, 5:17. | Uh huh. | Thanks.

What time is it, please? | Excuse me.

5

Okay, thanks. | No, I sure don't.

Excuse me, do you have the time? | Uh huh.

Unit 4: Sheet E

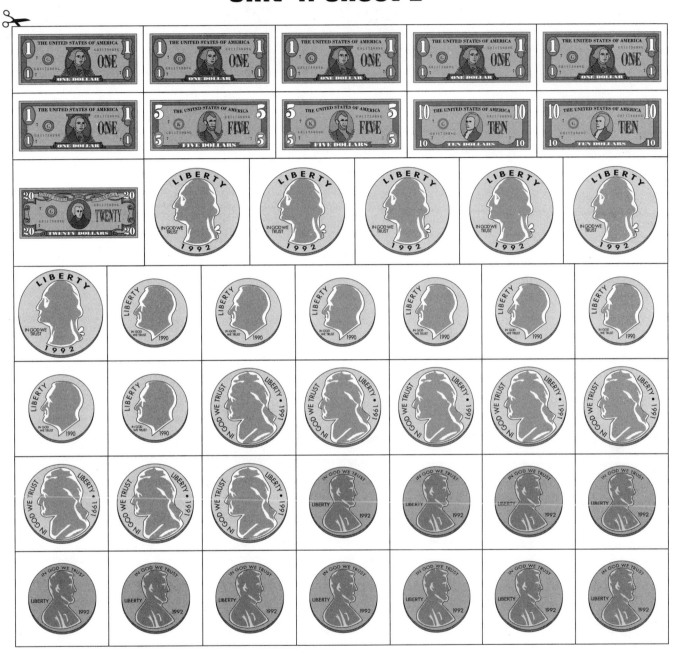

Unit 4: Sheet F

Sample

Thank you.	Sure.

Can I have change for a dollar?

1

Sure.	Thanks.	Bye.

Do you have two dimes and a nickel for a quarter?

2

Just, uh, five ones	Can I get change?

Sure, what do you need?

3

Five dollars, there you go.

Thank you.

Can I have change for five dollars?

There you go.

Can I get change for a dollar, please?

Okay.	Can I help you?	Thanks.

Unit 5: Sheet G

Sample

2864 Rose Avenue.	John Mack, M-A-C-K.

And the phone number?	Okay, and your address?

Your name, please?	446-8098.

1

544-2331.	Irma, I-R-M-A Ryan, R-Y-A-N.

Okay, the address, please.	Okay.

Phone number.	4374 Martin Drive.

Irma, I-R-M-A Ryan, R-Y-A-N.	Name, please.

2

And the phone number?	Grimsley, G-R-I-M-S-L-E-Y.

How do you spell your street?	And the name?

Michael Sanchez.	2837 Grimsley Avenue.

Area code 712 922-5837.	Address?

3

Kate Brosnan, B-R-O-S-N-A-N.	475 Bardin Road.

3-2, good, and your phone number?	And that's 748…?

Okay, and Kate, what is your address?	3-2.

Your name, please.	489-2357.

Unit 6: Sheet H

cheeseburger	hamburger	large coke	medium coke	small coke
large frostie	medium frostie	small frostie	onion rings	apple pie
cherry pie	milk	small fries	medium fries	large fries

Unit 6: Sheet J

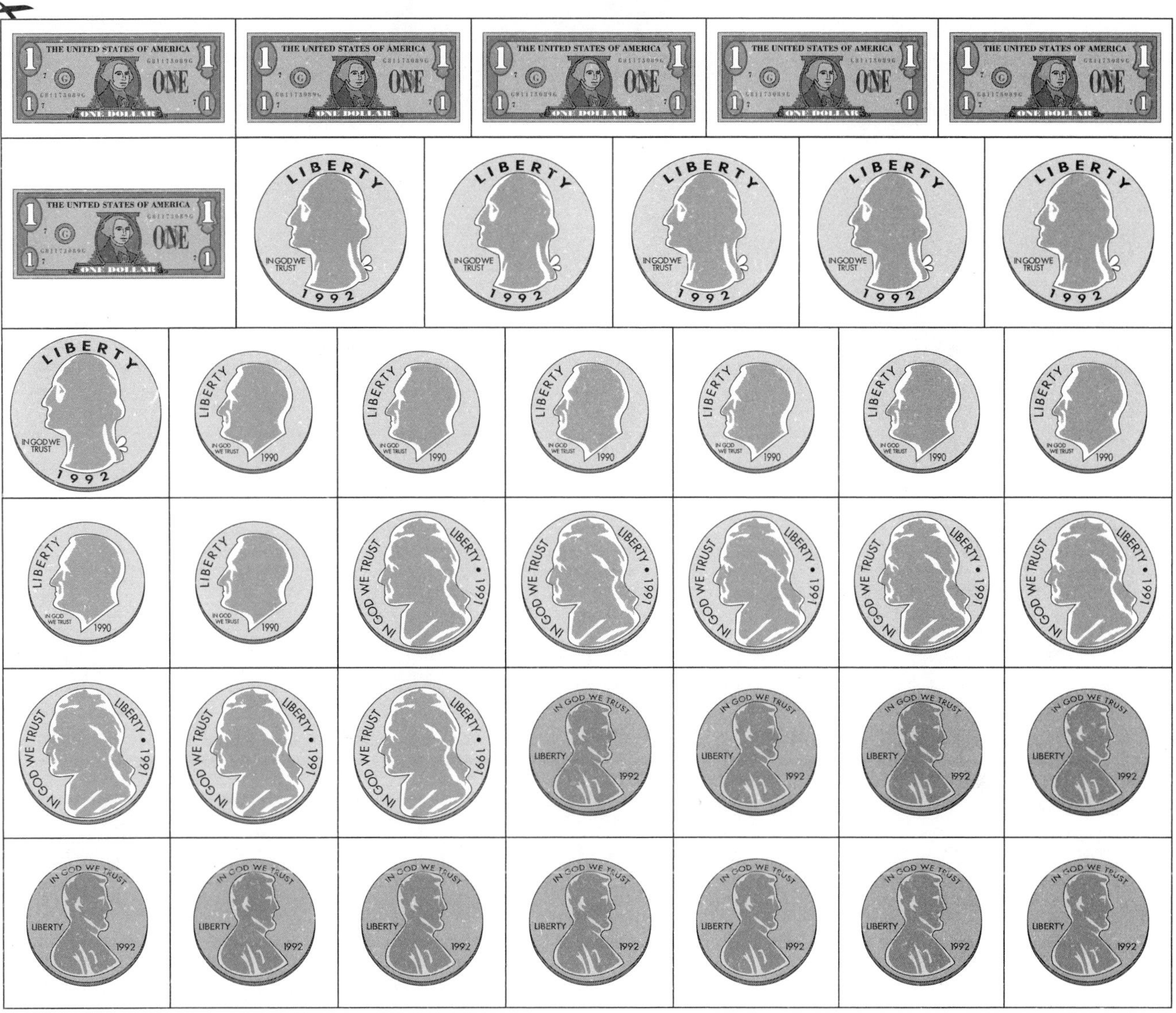

1

Can I help you, m'am?	$2.48, please.

Okay, I'll have a burger and fries.	For here.

Thank you.	Thank you.

Okay. For here or to go?	Okay.

2

For here.	Hi.

For here or to go?	And two medium cokes.

Will this be all?	One medium fries.

$2.69.	Okay.

3

Yes. Could I have a burger, small fries…	$4.20.

Hamburger, small fries…	and a coke.	Right.

For here or to go?	To go.	May I take your order?

Okay.	So you got a burger, small fries, and a coke.